CONTENTS

CHAPTER 1

DISTANCE

How far is far? A man jumped from 40 kilometres (25 miles) above Earth. A woman cycled 139,000 kilometres (86,500 miles) in one year. Scientists built a **space probe**. It is more than 21 billion km (13 billion miles) from Earth.

All of these feats are about distance.

Humans go as far as they can go.

Then they try to go just a little further.

People have set
distance feats
in many sports,
including cycling.

CHAPTER 2

THE MARIANA Trench

The Mariana **Trench** is the deepest part of the ocean. The tallest mountain on Earth could fit in it. There would still be room to spare.

James Cameron explored the trench in 2012. He used a submarine to travel 11 kilometres (6.8 miles) below the ocean's surface. It took him 2 hours and 36 minutes to reach the bottom.

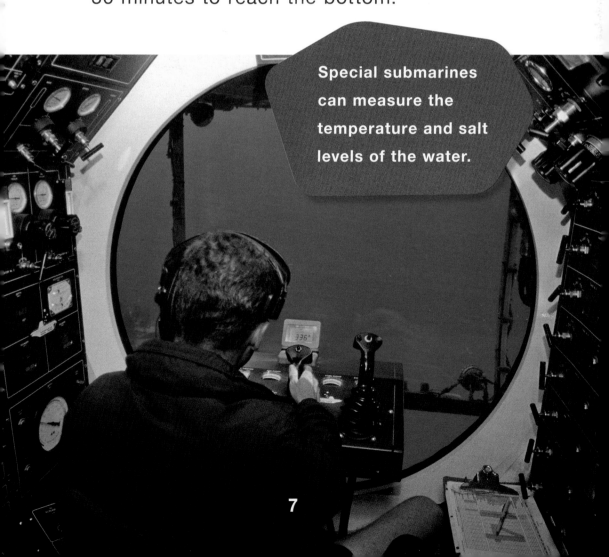

Special submarines can measure the temperature and salt levels of the water.

CHAPTER 3

A YEAR OF
Cycling

Amanda Coker started riding her bike in May 2016. She cycled around a park in Tampa, Florida, USA. The loop was 11 kilometres (7 miles) long.

Coker did not stop cycling. She kept cycling that loop. She cycled for 13 hours. She repeated that the next day. Then she repeated it for the next year.

Coker cycled an average of 378 km (235 miles) per day, all without leaving the city of Tampa.

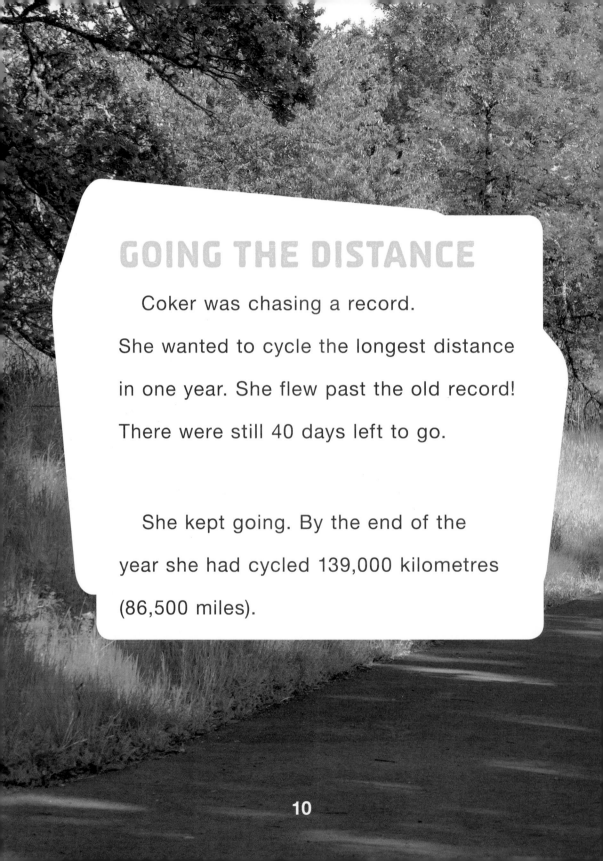

GOING THE DISTANCE

Coker was chasing a record.

She wanted to cycle the longest distance in one year. She flew past the old record! There were still 40 days left to go.

She kept going. By the end of the year she had cycled 139,000 kilometres (86,500 miles).

Coker cycled thousands of laps on a single path similar to this one.

AROUND THE WORLD

Coker's distance equals more than three trips around Earth!

CHAPTER 4

DIVING
Deep

Ahmed Gabr loves **scuba diving**. He is a deep-sea scuba diver from Egypt. He first learned to dive at the age of 18. He then taught the sport for almost 17 years. But teaching it wasn't enough. Gabr wanted to dive deeper than anyone else. He trained for four years to do so.

A scuba diver wears
an oxygen tank to
breathe underwater.

SET THE RECORD STRAIGHT

Ahmed Gabr dived into the

Red Sea in 2014. He dived

332 metres (1,090 feet). It took

him 12 minutes.

A scuba diver makes safety stops on his way back to the surface.

Coming up was the hard part.

Divers face changes in **pressure**.

These changes can cause sickness.

Coming up too fast can be deadly.

Gabr had to be careful.

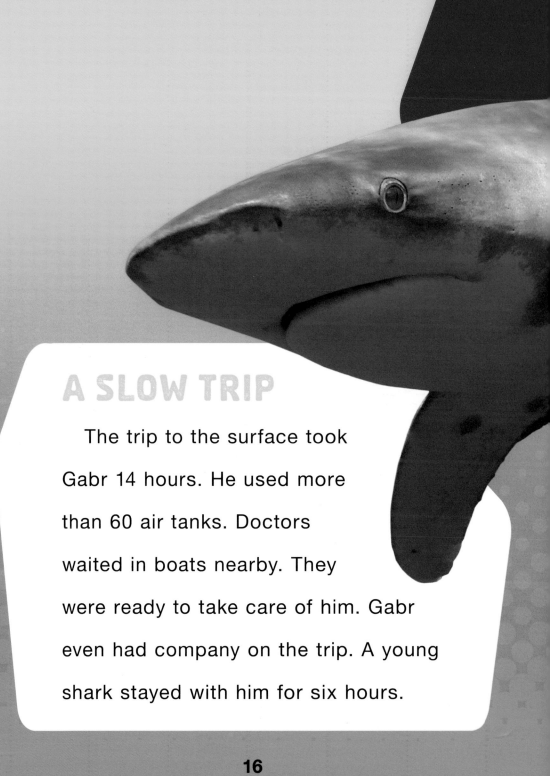

A SLOW TRIP

The trip to the surface took Gabr 14 hours. He used more than 60 air tanks. Doctors waited in boats nearby. They were ready to take care of him. Gabr even had company on the trip. A young shark stayed with him for six hours.

An oceanic whitetip
shark stayed with
Gabr as he rose
through the water.

Gabr was very happy when he surfaced. He beat the old record by 14.1 metres (46 feet). He set a new world record!

CHAPTER 5

FREE-FALLING

Alan Eustace wanted to **free-fall** further than anyone else. Scientists helped him to plan his trip. Eustace did it in 2014. He wore a special spacesuit.

Eustace travelled in a balloon to his final **altitude**. The balloon ride took two hours. He floated more than 40 kilometres (25 miles) above Earth.

A skydiver experiences a few seconds of free fall before she releases her parachute.

SUCH GREAT HEIGHTS

Eustace began his free fall. He fell 41,420 metres (135,890 feet). It took him only 15 minutes. He broke a world record. He fell from the highest height. His fastest speed was 1,323 km (822 miles) per hour. Eustace could see the darkness of space as he fell back to Earth.

RECORD HOLDER

Felix Baumgartner held the record before Eustace. He fell 39 km (128,100 feet) in 2012.

Eustace (left) wore a spacesuit that protected him against cold air and changes in air pressure.

CHAPTER 6

THE LONGEST
Jump

Stefan Kraft is a skier from Austria. He zoomed down a ramp in March 2017. The crowd roared as he flew. Kraft's skis finally touched down. He had jumped 253.5 metres (831.7 feet). It was the longest ski jump in history.

A skier must keep his body as straight as possible while in the air. This position increases distance.

CHAPTER 7

SPACE
Voyage

The US space programme sent out a space probe in 1977. The probe was called *Voyager 1*. Its job was to explore the planets. It flew past Jupiter in 1979. It passed Saturn in 1980. *Voyager 1*'s **mission** was over. But the probe kept going.

Voyager 1 launched on 5 September 1977.

A BILLION KILOMETRES AND COUNTING

Voyager 1 was still speeding out into space in 2012. It became the first man-made object to leave the solar system. The probe was more than 21 billion km (13 billion miles) from Earth in 2018. It gets further away every day. It still sends back data about space.

Voyager 1 carries a gold record. It has recordings of songs, animal calls and greetings in many languages. If life exists beyond Earth, it may find this record and learn a little bit about humans.

AMONG THE STARS

Voyager 1's next space encounter will be with a distant star – in 40,000 years.

GLOSSARY

altitude
height of an object above sea level

free-fall
move downwards under the force of gravity only

mission
task or job

pressure
continuous physical force on an object

scuba diving
sport in which a diver uses special gear to breathe underwater

space probe
robot designed to explore outer space

trench
long, narrow ditch

OTHER AMAZING FEATS

- In 2017, Luca Turrini of Australia set a record. He ran the greatest distance run on a treadmill in 24 hours. He ran more than 261 kilometres (162 miles).

- In 1970, the crew of *Apollo 13* flew past the dark side of the Moon. They were 400,171 kilometres (248,655 miles) from Earth. That is the furthest any human has been from Earth.

- In 2006, Veljko Rogoši of Croatia swam 225 kilometres (139.8 miles) across the Adriatic Sea. He swam the furthest distance in an open sea.

ACTIVITY

Try these distance challenges with your family and friends. You may need a tape measure to record the distances. You can also make up your own distance challenges.

- Make paper aeroplanes and throw them from a starting line. Who can throw the furthest?

- Start on a line and jump as far as you can. Who can jump the furthest?

- Go to a basketball court. Who can make the longest basketball shot?

FIND OUT MORE

Are you amazed by these distance feats and curious to find out more? Check out these resources:

Books

Audacious Aviators (Ultimate Adventurers), Jen Green (Raintree, 2014)

Courageous Circumnavigators (Ultimate Adventurers), Fiona Macdonald (Raintree, 2014)

Guinness World Records 2019 (Guinness World Records Ltd, 2018)

Jupiter and the Outer Planets (Astronaut Travel Guides), Andrew Solway (Raintree, 2013)

Websites

Take a virtual dive to the bottom of the Mariana Trench!
   www.bbc.co.uk/news/science-environment-17013285

Find out more about the *Voyager* mission.
   spaceplace.nasa.gov/voyager-to-planets/en/

INDEX